Boats Out of Water

How to haul out without breaking the bank or your boat!

Scott Wilson

A Lubber's Guide

ISBN: 978-0-9977760-4-1

Table of Contents

Introduction

If you own a boat any bigger than a runabout, hauling it out of the water can be a nerve-wracking experience. You hear the engines rev up on the Travelift, watch the straps tighten beneath the hull, and your imagination is off to the races. Did the straps land on a transducer? Will they crush it? What if they slip... up onto the prop shaft? The rudder? Or—and the second you think this, you can't *unthink* it—what if it *keeps sliding*... all the way out from under the boat?!? Is it going to drop back in the water? Onto the concrete? HALFWAY BETWEEN, SNAPPING THE HULL LIKE A TWIG!?!

You can hardly think about it. Maybe that haulout can wait for next year. Or, better yet, until after you sell the boat! The next owner can take care of it.

But somebody has to do it. That bottom isn't going to paint itself. You can only scrape and clean it in the water for so long before you're either down to the gelcoat or the barnacles become numerous enough to raise an army and fight back.

The frequency with which you haul out may vary according to your local conditions and personal predilections. In the Midwest, it's common for boats to be hauled every fall and stored on the hard to avoid the ice that clogs many marinas during the harsh winters there. In the Pacific Northwest, every two to three years is the norm.

Whatever the interval, sooner or later it's going to be *your* boat up in those straps. You'd better be ready for it!

PART ONE

Behind the Haulout

CHAPTER ONE

A Boat Out Of Water

Boats are beasts of the sea, but those of us who own and maintain them are not. We can dive, in warmer climates or in protective gear, for a limited time to scrape and scrub and screw and unscrew below the waterline, performing such maintenance as is possible in the watery realm. But you can't paint underwater, and woe unto him who tries to replace a thru-hull while the hole is still in the drink. You can dither and put it off, but sooner or later, that boat of yours is going to have to come out of the water.

You're not the first boater to face this truth. Haulouts were already a thing hundreds of years ago.

Careening was the traditional method for getting at the bottom. A soft beach was found, the vessel unceremoniously grounded, and when the tide went out, the crew went to work. Of course, they could only work on the high side and only while the tide was low enough. This made for a long, laborious, and dangerous process: neither grounding nor re-floating ships were controllable or safe.

Some of the work being done wasn't particularly safe, either... "graving"[1] involved lighting a fire beneath the careened hull to burn off weed and barnacle growth from the bottom. More than a few wooden boats were lost when the hull itself caught fire instead of just the weeds.

---

[1] From which we get the name "graving dock," or dry dock.

The ancient Chinese, as far back as 1088, realized that they needed to get at the hulls of some of their dragon ships to effect repairs to damages caused by the ravages of time ("...their hulls decayed and needed repairs, but the work was impossible as long as they were afloat."). They invented what may have been the very first graving docks to accomplish the work. History records that they then invented the world's first boathouse in a vain effort to keep the weather off the dragon ships and extend the amount of time until the next haulout was needed.[2]

In Europe, they hit on the idea of the dry dock a little bit later, but came up with an innovation that made their version enormously more useful: a floating structure that could be flooded and then raised beneath the vessel to be hauled out. The floating dry dock could be used anywhere and even towed from place to place, allowing work to occur where necessary, rather than just where the pit happened to be dug.

Over the years, other innovations have occurred in the haulout world: marine ways, boat lifts, slipways, and cranes, among others. And careening and tidal grids are still options for the adventurous or thrifty. But the basic necessity for hauling out hasn't seemed to have changed much. Every few years, just about every boat has to come out of the water for paint[3] and maintenance work.

---

[2] Needham, Joseph (1986). Science and Civilization in China: Volume 4 Part 3. Taipei: Caves Books, Ltd. Page 660

[3] A typo in the first draft had this as "pain." I almost decided to leave it that way.

CHAPTER TWO

Ways, Lifts, and Cranes

So how do you get a boat out of the water? You basically have two choices: lift the boat or drop the water out from under it.

There have been any number of crazy schemes for accomplishing this down through the centuries, but for small recreational vessels in modern times, those options have essentially been boiled down to ways, lifts, and cranes.

Marine Ways
Of the three, the least commonly used for small craft are marine ways.

Ways are a set of rails or skids run down a ramp into the water, along which a cradle runs. The boat is positioned over blocks fixed to the cradle that will support the hull and then secured. The cradle is pulled up the ramp until the cradle is dry.

This method of hauling out boats became a popular alternative to dry docks when railroad technology made it easy to build rails and rolling stock and to power them with steam engines. This reduced the construction difficulties and removed the timing of the haulout from the mercy of the tides.

Ways are still a popular way to launch or haul out larger vessels. The cradle in which the boat sits provides a lot of stability and can be rigged so as not to put excessive pressure on a part of the hull not designed to carry it. But many marine ways are fairly old now and they are becoming increasingly rare.

A subset of these, however, are still popular. Although they don't use rails, many yards make use of wheeled cradles or trailers (or launching trolleys, as they are sometimes called), usually towed by a truck or forklift, to raise and lower boats on a concrete ramp, or even a beach. These setups are quite common in undeveloped countries and still used for smaller vessels at some locations in the first world.

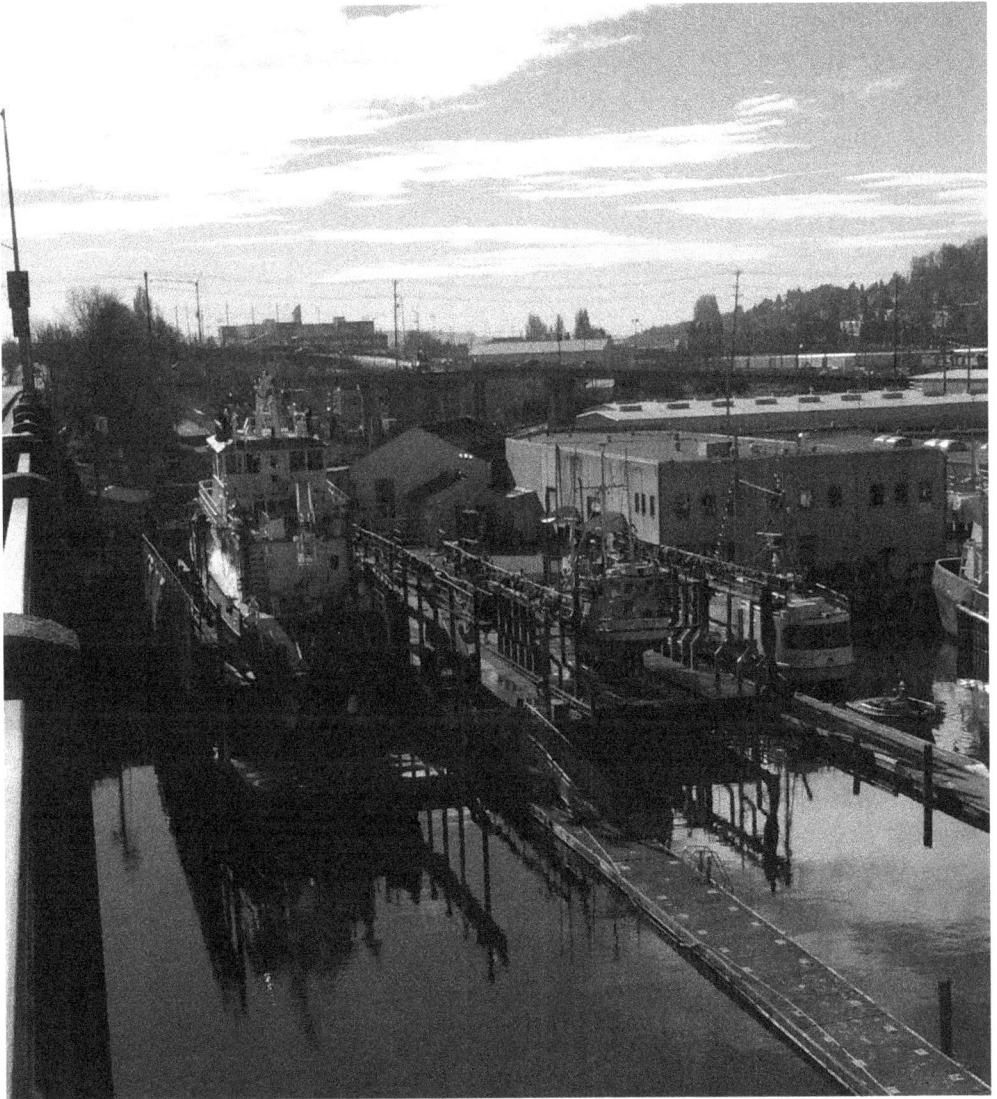

Two vessels hauled out on the marine ways at the Fishing Vessel Owner's Association on Seattle's Salmon Bay.

Travel Lifts

Travel lifts are simply a specialized sort of mobile crane. They are a wheeled, U-shaped box with sturdy straps extending between the legs of the U and attached to powerful winches.

The entire apparatus trundles out onto a pier, designed to match its shape, and lowers the straps into the open water beneath it. The boat then maneuvers into the open space, over the straps. The straps are then winched tight, drawing the boat up vertically until it is resting in the cradle of the lift. The lift can then drive itself, and the boat, anywhere in the yard, and lower the boat onto a cradle or jack stands, and then go back and get the next boat.

Travel lifts are typically very safe when operated competently, as the straps provide versatility in distributing the weight of the vessel evenly. Problems sometimes occur when the straps land on some underwater protrusion (a knotmeter paddlewheel, external coolers, a depth sensor) but the most common problems are, counterintuitively, with the hull above the waterline.

When operating properly, the breadth of the straps is sufficient to cradle the boat in a shallow "V" shape, with the straps separating from the topsides well before meeting the rub rail. When the lift is too narrow or the boat too wide (lay the blame where you will!), the straps may form more of a "U" shape, pinching hard against the rails and trying to fold the boat up like a taco.

A Travelift in action.

The geometry of the lift over the water can also impact this shape, with deeper drops from the pier to the water more likely to put a strain on the sides and rail. And a poorly positioned strap can stave in a porthole or crumple a propeller shaft in no time. Attentive operators will want to see a diagram or picture of your boat bottom before positioning the straps.

The versatility and speed of travel lifts has made them enormously popular with boat yards. The largest lifts can haul truly massive vessels—300 tons or more.

Forklifts

The convenience and maneuverability of the humble forklift makes it a popular choice for many haulout facilities today. The largest forklifts can pull boats almost 50 feet in length or weighing up to 50,000 pounds.

Forklifts have a more tricky balancing act to maintain than lifts, with the weight of the vessel out on a long lever arm from the center of gravity. Tales of operators accidentally nudging the forks open with the boat in the air are whispered with dread around waterfront bars.

Special consideration is necessary in determining where the forks will rest on the bottom of the hull and how the weight of the boat will settle when lifted. Since the forks are, typically, straight slabs of metal, while boat hulls are often delicately curved, this can result in one or two pressure points on each side of the vessel which bear the entirety of the weight when lifted. If the hull construction is not up to this load, the hull may be crushed.

Cranes

A simple tower crane may be one of the most straightforward ways to get a boat out of the water. A fixed crane on a pier or a mobile crane driven out onto one are both options, but both have significant limitations.

The fixed crane, obviously, can only pick boats up and sit them down next to where it is fixed. A cradle or some other device is required if the operator wants to have more than one boat out of the water at the same time.

A mobile crane must be deployed in one secure position while it is lifting, so it can't move boats around either, but at least it can go where the boat is. The limitations on mobile cranes have more to do with limited lifting capacity.

Cranes use straps, similar to travel lifts, and so share some of the same dangers with respect to positioning and potential damage to fittings or rails.

The Grid

There's another way to get at the bottom of your craft that doesn't involve any lifting at all. It harkens back to the olden days when the tide provided all the motive power required. Accordingly, it's called a tidal grid.

A tidal grid is usually nothing more than a stout set of timbers set along the bottom next to a pier or other apparatus for securing the boat. The boat is brought in and tied up to the pier on a high tide sufficient to clear the bottom of the grid; then you wait for a low tide low enough to expose the bottom of the boat for the work required.

This has an advantage over careening in that the boat doesn't need to be heeled over and is supported on her keel. Both sides of the hull are accessible.

On the other hand, it shares some of the same disadvantages as careening: you are at the mercy of the weather and tides. There's no possibility of tenting over the boat to work on it. You can always wait for better weather, but it needs to coincide with the proper tide. And any task that takes longer than the tidal cycle is right out the window.

Nor should you be grinding, scraping, or painting, or taking on any other task that will shower pollutants directly onto the sea bottom. There's no way to capture and process such stuff on a grid.

For a quick check of the prop or a fast keel repair in an out-of-the-way place, a tidal grid can be just the thing.

CHAPTER THREE

Picking the Yard

In some parts of the world, you may not have a lot of options when it comes to picking a boat yard to haulout at; there may only be one nearby! Or, perhaps you are having work performed exclusively by a particular large service center. They'll do the work in their own yard, so there is no choice for you to make after picking the company itself.

If you're hoping to do much of the work yourself or plan on hiring a variety of independent contractors, then you may have a few different options to choose between. There are several factors to consider as you are making this choice.

Who Will Do The Work

This question essentially boils down to whether or not you will be doing most or all of the work yourself, or if you will be paying someone else to do it.

As a sort of reverse of the situation where you pick a business with its own yard and they require that you haul out there in order for them to perform the work, if you pick a yard owned by a certain business, they may require that you use them to do the work. For business, liability, and environmental reasons, some companies simply won't let anyone other than their own employees work in their yard.

More commonly, boatyards may have a list of approved vendors. These are businesses that have arranged permissions to perform work in the yard despite not being a part of the company that owns it. In these situations, boat owners may or may not be allowed to do the work themselves. Other vendors can often obtain permission to come in and work on a particular project on a particular boat. In either case, you simply need to arrange matters with the yard boss.

Finally, there is the good old-fashioned open boatyard... the wild west of yards. Anyone walking in off the street can pick up tools and sand, grind, drill, or paint away to their heart's content. You can do your own work there, or hire someone to come in and help you, or any combination as you see fit.

This doesn't mean that those yards are completely without rules—almost nowhere is, these days—but anyone who can comply with them will be allowed to work on their boat there.

How The Work Will Be Done

Yard owners want to ensure that work is done in a safe and compliant manner. One way to exercise that oversight is by only allowing vendors who have proven they can do the job properly. Many of the restrictions on who can do what work where stem from environmental compliance and liability concerns.

There's always more than one way to paint a cat (as in catamaran... get it?), though, and in the wide world of marine engineering, everyone seems to have their own individual opinion about which way is best. If you—or your chosen vendor—have a strong opinion about the methods that must be used with your boat, then you need to make sure to pick a yard that is okay with you doing it that way.

If, for example, you need to strip your bottom paint down to the gelcoat, a common method is sandblasting. But blasting generates a lot of airborne pollutants, and many yards won't allow you to do it out in the open. Even tenting the vessel may not be enough. If sandblasting is your preference, you'll have to find a yard that can accommodate it.

On the other hand, chemical strippers are also used to take bottom paint off and create less airborne contaminants. If you're willing to go that route, many yards will allow it with nothing more than extra tarps down to catch the runoff.

The Busy Season

If your area has a definable boating season, then the shoulder seasons are likely to be the busiest time for most yards. You might find yourself waiting a long while for a date with the lift if you don't reserve a slot early. Vendors, likewise, will be busy as many other owners rush to either commission their boats for cruising or decommission them for storage.

The flip side of this is that you can often score good deals if you are willing to deal with any inconvenience associated with hauling out in the off-season. Many yards run specials or offer discounted rates to stay busy during the slow parts of the year.

But there are sometimes reasons those parts of the year are slow. Inclement weather can make work difficult or impossible.

If you are far enough north, in your region it may be the norm to haul out for the winter and leave the boat on the hard. There are a number of advantages to doing this when temperatures dip below freezing and waterways ice up for long periods since it makes winterizing the vessel more convenient. It can also be an advantage for performing regular maintenance work since the boat is already out of the water.

Due to the climate, though, you will almost certainly be restricted to performing any exterior work in early fall or late spring… the same time as everybody else. On the other hand, the yards will be used to this and usually have the capacity to get everyone back in the water in a timely manner.

Pricing and Convenience

Looking at a bill from some boatyards can be like trying to decipher Fermat's Last Theorem. There are complicated equations, adjustments, unexplained fees, and sometimes outright perversions of normal mathematical principles.

In general, the yard will charge you a fixed amount (usually based on the length of your boat) for a round-trip haulout on the lift, and a daily charge for each day you are out (called lay-days).

On top of those charges, there may be regional environmental fees, charges for using the wash-down station, taxes, labor charges, and other costs.

It's best if you try to get some bids before you pick your yard, but estimating yacht repair is an imprecise science. There is always something uncovered during the actual process of repairs that will throw the numbers off.

Accessibility

Another factor to consider, for your convenience and that of the yard, is the dimensions of the boat. Every method of lifting a boat has limitations on weight and dimensions. Check your owner's manual to ensure that you have the correct figures for your vessel. You will need to know your LOA, or length overall (and quite possibly the Extreme Length of Vessel, or ELOV, which is the total distance between the forward-most and aft-most appendages on the boat, including sprits, davits, etc.), beam, weight, and draft.

The yard operator will probably ask you for this information when you schedule the haulout, but if they don't, confirm for yourself that they can handle your size of boat.

Another consideration for some people is whether or not the yard allows you to stay on board while on the hard. Some places simply do not have the facilities for this; others say they don't allow it for liability reasons but may wink and nod at the practice. And still others are very accommodating to livea-boards.

Reputation

There is no substitute for experience when it comes to pick-ing a good yard and vendors, but reputation can be a big help. Will the yard take advantage of the fact that they have you over a barrel, or will their adjustments be reasonable and objective? As you ask around, you'll no doubt find other boaters in your area who have formed some firm opinions about which yard managers are known to be a little sharp in their dealings. Some of this will be after-action grousing that comes with any unex-pectedly large bill, deserved or not. But if you start hearing the same yard repeatedly mentioned in the negative column, don't let the fact that some people have had a good experience there dissuade you. The reputation becomes important when things go sideways, not when they go as planned.

Even after you check around and get an idea how different yards are regarded, it pays to go take a walk around and check them out before you decide. Just watching the yard staff at work can tell you quite a lot about whether or not to trust them with your boat.

- Watch how they haul out a few other vessels. Do they:
  - Secure the slings or straps to prevent them sliding along the hull?
  - Drive the lift prudently, without swinging the boats around a lot?
- Look at the blocking of vessels already on the hard
  - Are the jack stands secured to prevent slippage?
  - Is the blocking beneath the keel robust and in good condition?

While you're there, chat with some of the crew or other folks there working on boats. You'll get a sense for how things are run pretty quickly… and whether or not it's the right yard for you.

PART TWO

Preparing to Haul Out

CHAPTER FOUR

Planning

A well-planned haulout is a happy haulout! You can look around any boatyard for a wealth of counter examples: boats in various states of disrepair, racking up yard fees awaiting parts that weren't ordered on time, missing splash dates, accumulating layers of yard dust, and generally not serving their primary purpose of allowing their owners to get out and have fun on the water.

Planning your haulout can involve a lot of different variables, but there is one firm and unyielding truth to which you must adhere: don't go back in the water with any unplugged holes in the bottom of your boat!

Tasks

Since haulouts are expensive, and grow more expensive the longer they last, there is a lot of pressure to get many different tasks accomplished in the time allotted. You will want to start just by drawing up a list of everything that you hope to accomplish while your boat is out of the water.

Don't try to get this all done in one sitting. You will find that new tasks come to mind randomly and at odd hours as your mind mulls over the job ahead of you. Just jot them down. You may consult the Appendix: Common Yard Tasks to see if there is anything on that list that jogs your memory.

Once stuff stops popping into your head, it's time to organize the list.

Priorities

There can be three different categories of tasks on your list:

- Jobs that are impossible to perform when the boat is in the water.
- Jobs that are *difficult* to perform in the water, but would still be possible.
- Jobs that can be performed in the water, but would still be easier when hauled out.

So those are the broad categories you should start with. Sort out all the different tasks into those three groups. Anything that can be done in the water and is not easier in the yard shouldn't be on the list at all.

Those groups give you your overall priorities. The things that absolutely *must* be done in the yard will be the most important. When it comes down to a question of where to put your re-sources, the jobs in that group should get love first. Make sure you have all those supplies ordered early, get whatever help you will need lined up, make sure the necessary tools are read-ily available.

You may want to sort things within those three categories, too. If you have a job that is likely to be time-consuming or which may uncover additional unknown problems, plan to tackle that first. If there is a task that you know will be hard, you should probably schedule it early on, when you have the energy and wherewithal to get through it.

If you're doing it right, when you get down to the wire the only things left to do will be things that you *could* do after you get back in the water. If you have time to take care of them while you're in the yard, then that's just a bonus.

Checklists

Your time in the yard will probably be hectic. There will be a lot of projects to demand your attention and many of them will go fractal on you: pull the propeller off the shaft and discover that you have a worn cutless bearing, perhaps. Or you go to torque down your keel bolts and discover an electrolysis issue that has eaten the threads out of the nuts. There are always fresh problems hiding under problems you already knew about. When you find them, you will have to fix them (perhaps; see Contingencies for a discussion about leaving well enough alone), and this can radically change your day from the way you thought it was going to go.

When this happens, it's easy to lose track of your priorities. Or perhaps you will have to change them. In either case, you need a reference you can come back to again and again to ensure you are still on track to accomplish everything that you need to accomplish while you are out of the water.

Enter the humble checklist.

Checklists are a fine thing aboard boats at any time, but they are particularly valuable when stress levels are high, as they are during a haulout. No matter what tricks your brain plays on you, what diversions you are launched on by unexpected discoveries, you can always look down at that slip of paper and see that, no, indeed, you have not yet secured the propeller shaft nut.

Checklists can be as detailed or vague as you might like based on personal preference. Maybe, for you, it's enough to just check off that final mark at the end of the job:

▫ Head intake thru-hull replaced

Or maybe you would prefer to make sure you hit all the steps along the way. You might end up with something like this:

▫ Order new intake valve and thru-hull
▫ Replace head intake thru-hull
 - Remove old thru-hull assembly
  - Remove mounting flange nuts
  - Remove seacock
 - Fabricate new mounting ring
 - Dry fit new thru-hull assembly

- Secure new flange with mounting nuts
- Insert and tighten seacock
- Seal mounting nuts
- Seal new fitting
- Mount tailpiece

It's entirely up to you how detailed or basic you want to make your lists, but keeping some sort of checklist is highly recommended. In the stress of time spent in the yard and with the clock ticking, it's all too easy to forget something important or expensive if you didn't bother to write it down first!

Finally, you'll need to line up all the tools and supplies required to accomplish everything on your list. That's a big enough job that it gets its own chapter.

Planning with Vendors

If you are going to have contractors take care of the work, you will still need to do some planning, but it will be a different sort of planning process. You won't need to figure out the step-by-step details. Instead, you will need to make sure that you are setting down clear expectations about the work you want done and how it should be done (if that is of concern to you—and it should be!).

It can be difficult to get vendors to engage with you on project planning. Many have been in business working on boats for a long time. They probably know a lot more about boat work than you do. They might think it is a waste of their time for you to insist on discussing the details of the work with them—a sign of distrust.

On the other hand, some vendors will avoid such conversations on another basis—that it can expose the fact that they *don't* know what they are doing.

Insist on working with contractors who are willing to discuss their process with you and patient enough to explain it to your satisfaction.

Since you are paying for the work, it's also reasonable (though sometimes futile) to discuss cost estimates. But both because contractors are as human and as innately optimistic as the rest of us, and because of the aforementioned fractal nature of boat projects, it's common for these to be wildly inaccurate.

More important than an estimate, then, is to make the contractor aware of your budget. If you only have a certain amount to spend on a project, tell them up front what that number is. It's true that this can harm your position if you are attempting to negotiate a price, since you have just disclosed your bottom line number. On the other hand, it's a powerful incentive for vendors to not delve too deeply into work that you have signaled you are unable to pay them for.

Get a clear agreement on go/no-go points in the work process where the contractor should stop and contact you if it looks like time or costs are going to go off the rails. The natural inclination for marine professionals is to fix problems that they find. But this can lead into a neverending cycle of expensive work that keeps your boat in the yard far past what you had planned. You might prefer to defer some of that work, even if it costs more to fix later, just to get out on the water on schedule. Or perhaps not, but the point is that it should be your *choice* to proceed or not with unplanned jobs, not a *fait accompli* presented by a mechanic who decided to fix that little ticking sound when he was just supposed to be replacing your filters.

Insist on a call and giving your explicit approval for any work not previously discussed.

CHAPTER FIVE

Preparation

Once you have your plans sketched out, you can make executing them a lot easier with some pre-haulout preparation.

We'll talk about lining up your supplies in the next section. It's time to get both yourself and the boat ready for the work you will be doing.

You and The Yard

Hopefully, you're not going to be spending too much time in the boatyard, but no matter what your plan is, it's a good idea to go visit the yard and have a chat with the staff a few days before your lift. Familiarize yourself with:

- Lift procedures—how to position the vessel and at what point you will get off
- Blocking standards
- The location, if known, where your boat will be placed
- Environmental standards

If they can tell you the spot you will be going, check your access to water and electrical. Will you need an adapter to connect to power?

If you are having the yard do the work, you can also discuss your expectations in more detail with the workers who will actually be performing the tasks. If you feel your spidey senses tingling about anyone's lack of expertise or motivation, now is the time to raise those questions with management.

This is also as good a time as any to dig out any diagrams or photos you have of the boat below the waterline and go over them with the lift operators. If there is going to be a problem with a thru-hull location or other appendage, it's better to hear about it long before you are motoring into the lift.

Preparing The Boat

You can also make life easier by prepping the boat itself as much as possible before you actually get it out of the water. Remember, you are paying for your time in the yard—don't waste it with tasks that you could have gotten out of the way while still in the water.

At a minimum, it's a good idea to clean and stow the interior securely and prep your decks as if you were going to sea. The ride out of the water will probably be smooth, but there may be some swinging and jostling and a few unexpected angles along the way. Don't be the guy that accidentally loses his stern anchor between the wash-down pit and the blocks. They'll be telling that story around the yard breakroom for years.

Secure portholes and hatches. This is more about keeping out dust and grime than keeping anything in. Yards are dirty places and the more you can keep on the outside of the boat, the less cleaning you will have to do when all is said and done.

If you are going to need access to any interior spaces of the hull for the work you plan to do, see about getting them open and accessible ahead of time. Remove any panels or gear that might get in the way.

While you're moving stuff out of the way, think about taking some of it off the boat for the duration of your stay. Any gear or tools that would be in the way may not need to live on board during the haulout. Anything of value might be safer elsewhere, too—yards are one-stop shopping for thieves.

Consider draining water and sewage tanks before you come out. You don't need that extra weight for anything, and the fluids in them can only cause problems while you are out of the water.

CHAPTER SIX

Supplies

Almost everything you might do in a boatyard will require supplies of some sort. These might be replacement parts, maintenance items, or tools.

There are few things more frustrating than starting in on a job that you have hauled out for only to find that you don't have the tools you need to finish it.

So you will want to get your supplies lined up ahead of time… well ahead of time, if possible. Although boating is a big industry, it's not anywhere close to the scale of, say, housing. Consequently, there are fewer suppliers and specialized goods and equipment are more expensive and may be harder to find. So the lead times for ordering and receiving supplies might be longer than you are accustomed to in our modern world of online ordering and overnight delivery.

This crunch becomes particularly noticeable just before boating season gets underway. You and several thousand other boaters are all suddenly in a rush to get ready for fun out on the water and the demand shrinks inventories and puts a strain on shipping departments at major vendors.

If you can beat the rush, you'll be sure to have all your important supplies in hand while other boaters are still watching futilely out the window for the UPS guy to show up.

Supplies and Suppliers

Everyone knows that marine-grade goods are more expensive and harder to find than regular household items. But it is not always quite so clear what exactly "marine-grade" means or whether that designation is worth the extra cost.

Experience will have to be your guide when deciding between purpose-built nautical supplies and relying on something from Home Depot. But in the interest of saving both time and money, it's often worth checking out your local hardware store to see if they have what you need before you make the trek to the chandlery. They are more likely to have stock on hand, and it will probably be less expensive. In many cases, it may literally be the same item you would find at a chandler.

On the other hand, there can be added value in shopping at your local chandler. There are many aspects to marine product selection and installation that don't apply in conventional environments. An experienced chandler has dealt with thousands of customers and heard all the stories. They probably have a very good idea about the challenges you will be facing and can offer tips and tricks to make your haulout tasks much easier.

Ultimately, your best bet is simply to make time to shop around before you haul out and evaluate your options before laying in your supplies.

Things to consider when purchasing from non-marine vendors:

- **Waterproofing** - Truly marinized products will have waterproofing where goods designed for land use might not. Check the details when you are comparison shopping.
- **Metals** - Not all stainless steel is created equal! Be sure you're getting the grade you need. And mixing dissimilar metals can speed corrosion.
- **Warranties** - Some products are expressly not warrantied for marine environments.

Even when working with specialty marine products, not all are created equal. Many vendors target the recreational market, which may not be as demanding as that for commercial mariners. Many experienced boaters look to the suppliers used by tugs, fishing vessels, and other vessels that make a living on the water—the engineering (and cost!) tends to be more robust than with products aimed at the recreational boating market.

Last Minute Supplies

Of course, haulouts are full of surprises and last minute adjustments. You probably will not be able to predict all the supplies you will need down to the last detail. At some point, you'll find yourself desperately running around to every chandler in town, looking for a particular and rare prop nut you hadn't known you were going to need.

There's nothing you can do about what you don't know. What you can do is be prepared for that desperate last minute search when it comes at you.

Getting Ready for Last Minute Supply Runs

You can be ready by making a survey of potential suppliers, local and remote, before you begin the haulout. A few weeks before, as you are shopping for the items you know you will need, take the time to drive around to all those local shops (assuming you aren't already familiar with them) and do a little browsing. Get a feel for the prices and the stock levels. Chat with the staff—how fast can they get rush orders delivered? What are the costs for speedy delivery? Who are their suppliers and how are their relationships with those suppliers?

All these factors can impact your ability to get unusual items at the last minute. You will probably find some shop or another has better pricing, or a wider variety of items on hand, or just gives you a better vibe for being helpful and service-oriented. That's going to be your first stop on that urgent last minute parts run.

You can also check out Internet-based suppliers on a similar basis. Read up on their deadlines and charges for overnight delivery. What do their return policies look like? It's possible you might actually be able to get parts faster from the Internet than a local shop since the Internet-based retailers are experienced with and optimized for shipping.

PART THREE

In The Yard

CHAPTER SEVEN

Getting a Lift

Preparation and Arrival

You can make your life a lot easier in the yard by getting your boat ready ahead of time.

- Secure your rigging and sails, if you have a sailboat— many people remove their sails and stow them. Loose sails and high winds have tipped more than one boat off the stands!
- Empty your bilge and disable any bilge pumps.
- Secure the interior for sailing—you may get jostled a bit getting onto the lift, and the boat may not be blocked completely level in the yard.
- Consider removing your knotmeter and replacing it with a plug, if possible. These delicate instruments can easily be crushed by slings or blocks.
- Secure your decks—loose lines, fenders, and other debris can come off and get tangled in yard equipment, to everyone's great regret.

Don't be late to your lift date!

Most yards have docks where you can tie up temporarily while waiting for your turn at the lift. Make sure you are not obstructing access to the lift point. Someone else may be coming out ahead of you, or another boat may have to go into the water before yours can come out.

Liftoff

Different yards have different procedures and rules. Talk the process over with the workers if you are unsure. Some operators will want you off the boat before it comes out; others will have you stay on board to maneuver into position and have you step off when the deck is even with the pier.

A sailboat in the lift slings; notice that the slings are strapped together so they cannot slip apart and drop the boat in between. Garbage bags are

also taped to the canvas slings above the waterline level to protect the hull gelcoat—signs of an attentive yard.

A yard worker should come chat with you about how to position their forks or straps on the underside of your hull. It is extremely useful if you have a picture or diagram from previous haulouts to illustrate. Your concern will be that the process not damage anything on your hull; the yard will want to position things to adequately support the weight and stabilize the boat as it comes out and travels to its ultimate destination.

You will have to trust the yard workers as they do their job—this is why you researched the reputation of the yard ahead of time! But it's always a good sign to see Travelift operators who pad their slings to avoid scratching your gelcoat, and who tie the fore and aft straps together so they can't pull apart and drop your boat like an egg.

For larger vessels, some yards use multiple straps for better weight distribution and security.

Almost every yard has pressure sprayers on hand to blast marine gunk off the bottom of boats coming out. Some will let you do the spraying yourself and some will charge you for yard workers to do it. It's increasingly common for this to be done at a special washdown pit where the runoff water is collected for processing, lest pollutants run back into the ocean.

A dab hand with the spray gun can save you a lot of scraping later on if you have a lot of growth on the bottom, so don't blow past this step. Some washers are even powerful enough to take off some of the paint. If you are putting on a fresh coat (and you should be!), this is a benefit and you should clear as much of the old stuff off as you can. If you want to leave it on, be careful! You could be looking at naked gelcoat if you get too aggressive.

Blocking
Blocking is another art of the yard that you have to hope the workers have mastered.

A properly blocked-up sailboat in the yard.

In the water, your boat is supported by buoyant forces that push "up" equally on every underwater part of the hull. Out of the water, it will be resting on a few points, greatly increasing the amount of weight those points will have to bear.

Typically, the greater part of the weight rests on the keel, a beefy member that should be up to the task. Workers will build a lumber crib to set the keel on, then balance the boat with jack stands or other cribbing to form a solid platform beneath it.

Depending on your boat and the yard, it's nice to see the stands secured so they can't slip out of place. This makes it slightly more difficult to access the bottom (usually, a chain is strung between the stands, holding them in tension with one another) but much safer!

Although yard workers will do their best to block your boat safely and securely, they can't be expected to be familiar with every detail of construction for every model of vessel. It's up to you to verify that your keel and hull can accommodate the weight of the vessel and to know about any places that will be damaged if they are used as support points. If you have concerns about how the vessel should be blocked, talk to the yard staff before they pull your boat out.

CHAPTER EIGHT

Painting

Although there are a lot of different reasons to haul out, almost every haulout involves some painting. For many boat owners, this is the primary reason to haul out. But even for those with other goals, it's rare to pass up an opportunity to slap another coat of paint on as long as the boat is already out of the water. Few proactive maintenance jobs are as easy, inexpensive, or worthwhile as a bottom paint job.

Paint goes on easy after careful preparation.

Preparation

Any painter will tell you that the key to a good paint job is in the preparation, not the painting itself. Preparing a surface that paint will adhere to, while ensuring that adjacent spots *not* to be painted are protected, is the most time-consuming but important parts of putting on a bottom paint job.

There are two general types of paints used on saltwater hulls:[4]

- **Ablative** - Gradually sheds layers through scrubbing or the action of water against the hull, exposing fresh layers of biocide[5] and carrying away marine growth.
- **Hard** - Remains intact on the bottom of the boat, slowly leaching out biocide content to discourage growth.

Some hybrid paints which combine the qualities of both hard and ablatives are available now also, but for most preparation purposes they can be lumped together with regular ablatives. It's vitally important to know which kind of paint your boat has on it currently before you start applying a fresh coat.

It's possible to apply ablative paint over hard paint, but not the other way around... the hard coat will just flake off as the lower ablative coat does what it's designed to do.

Equally important is your hull material. Copper-based paints, for instance, should never be used on aluminum hulls—the metals are dissimilar enough to create severe galvanic corrosion issues.

---

[4] Although barnacles and other sea creatures do not grow in fresh water, boats that are left in freshwater can also benefit from being painted. Most lake sailors favor a low copper-content hard paint for low-maintenance and effective deterrence of slime and scum growth.

[5] A substance designed to poison or repel organisms that grow on hulls; often metal-based, but increasingly composed of more environmentally friendly chemicals. Of course, since the environment itself is the problem, finding an effective but friendly formulation is challenging.

Different formulations are found to be effective in different water conditions. You'll want to check around with other local sailors to find what is most common in your area. In general, any paint with a high biocide content is going to be more effective than one with a lower content.

In the past, biocides have primarily consisted of various sorts of lethal heavy metals, originally copper, then tin as it was found to be more effective, and then copper again as tin was found to be *too* effective. The very fact that those metals are poisonous to marine life makes them environmentally unfriendly. Current trends are to deploy biocides that are generally less toxic.

The jury is still out on the most effective formulation, or indeed whether or not such biocides can truly replace copper and tin. Your best bet is to consult the most current research and check around with other boaters in your area for practical experience.

The worst part of painting a boat hull is usually removing the old paint.

If your hull has a relatively solid layer of the right type of paint on it already, with good adhesion, then a couple passes with a random orbit sander with 80-grit paper might be the only thing you need to do. If the paint is flaking away, has a thick buildup, or is the wrong kind of paint for you to paint over, then you have a lot more work ahead of you.

Scraping and sanding can handle much of the job, but if you genuinely need to get all the old paint off, then you are looking at a much harder and longer job, which may require professional assistance.

Sandblasting is one way to get the hull surface down to the gelcoat without damaging it. Chemical strippers are another alternative. Both can be extremely messy and dangerous to handle, and most yards will have special rules for controlling the resulting waste.

Taping and Tenting

Once you get the old paint off, you have to make sure that the new coat you are going to put on won't end up in places you don't want it—your topsides, for example, or running gear.

Taping at the waterline with regular masking tape will protect your topsides. Make the tape strip as broad as you are sloppy. Make sure the edge is sealed tight, so bubbles don't allow paint to siphon up over the waterline. Plan to remove the tape when the paint is still wet or tacky—you'll get a cleaner line and no flaking as you pull it off.

If rain seems likely, you can put a tape "gutter" along the waterline also by bending away the lower half of the tape, so water runs away and drips off instead of continuing down the hull. This won't defend against a heavy downpour but can get you through light showers or sprinkles without pause.

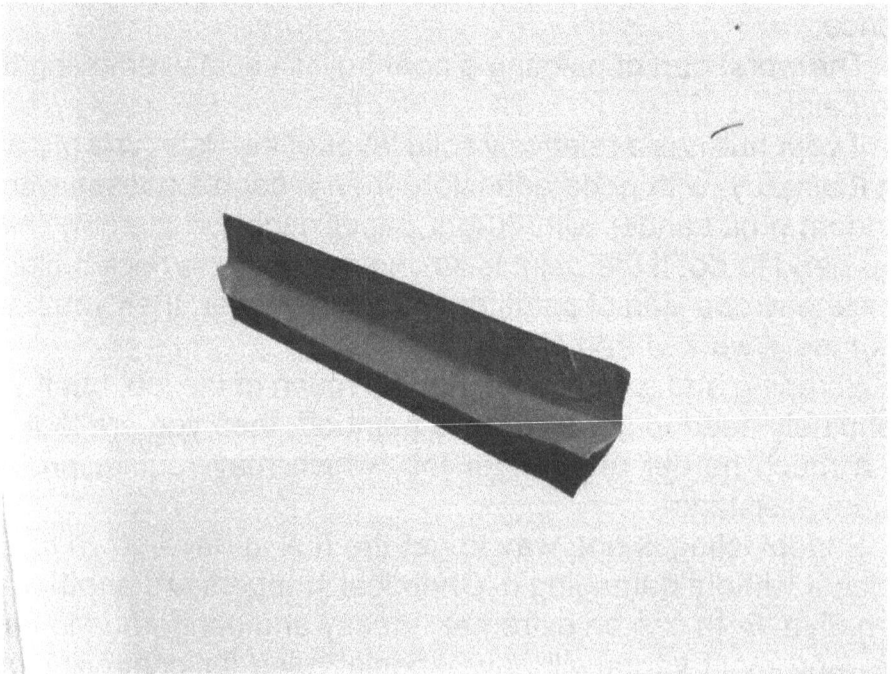

An example of a tape gutter; rain running down the hull will drip off the lip and not run through fresh paint.

If you have more serious environmental challenges, you may have to tent around the boat. Although this process looks like it should be easy—just drape plastic sheeting off the deck, right?—in practice it requires some planning and construction work to pull off.

Even though it involves extra work at the beginning, you are usually better off making a frame to tack the sheeting to instead of just trying to drape it. Otherwise, loose edges of the plastic will blow around, slapping wet paint around or tearing away entirely.

Painting

Actually slapping the paint on the bottom will come as a relief after all the trouble of the prep work. Coats will go on quickly, and the bottom will look smooth and beautiful. You'll hate putting such a work of art back in the water where no one can admire it!

Just before you paint, wipe down the bottom with acetone to get rid of any paint dust or other detritus left over from sanding.

Follow the directions given with your paint carefully with respect to times for drying and re-coating. Temperature will have a marked impact on the length of time required for drying between coats or before you can go back in the water.

Some folks start at the waterline and work their way down while others start at the keel and work up. The major advantage of going from low to high is that the odds of dragging your hair through wet bottom paint are dramatically decreased. But other folks paint in stripes, moving fore and aft, which also helps to avoid this issue.

For most hulls, rolling is the way to go since there are long, open stretches that a roller will make quick work of. But you will also need some brushes on hand for detail work around thru-hulls, sensors, shafts, and rudders.

Some paints also have only a limited amount of time that they can be *out* of the water. The copper in hard, epoxy-based paints deteriorates with exposure to air. So if you plan to be out of the water for a couple months, painting might best be scheduled near the end.

You will encounter certain practical obstacles during painting, namely the jack stands and bracing holding the boat up. Many yards will reposition the jack stands for you for free or for a small charge. Put on one coat and then have them moved before the next coat—this ensures that at least one coat goes on all the way around. A piece of wax paper inserted between the stand and the freshly painted hull (wait until it's dry to move the stands) will keep from scuffing the paint.

There's less you can do about any cribbing beneath the boat, although it may be possible to reblock the vessel entirely. This will involve a lift and more expense. Most yards instead will give you a few minutes grace to touch up the spots on the bottom of the keel and hull where the cribbing was located just before you go back in the water. This isn't ideal, since it almost certainly won't allow sufficient drying time, but it's better than nothing!

Other Regular Maintenance

Painting is the most common haulout task, but it's not the only part of regular maintenance you should attend to. There are a few other quick and inexpensive jobs that you should probably perform at almost every haulout to keep your boat afloat and in great shape.

Change the Anodes

Any boat with metal bits protruding beneath the water is susceptible to galvanic corrosion. This is an electrochemical process whereby two metals with different electrode potentials either come into direct contact or are connected by an electrolytic chemical—say, seawater—where the metal with the lower potential leaks ions to the metal of the higher potential. This weak electrical flow gradually degrades the structure of the *anode* (the metal with the lower potential) and can cause enormous damage to your engine, propeller, metal thru-hulls or hulls.

But this process can also be used to protect those same structures by attaching an even *lower* potential metal to them, called a sacrificial anode. Since you can't prevent electrolysis from occurring in water, you can at least ensure it happens to a bit of metal you don't care about.

Zinc is so commonly used for this purpose that most anodes are just called "zincs." They are often attached to propeller shafts as a sort of collar, or as large slabs on other metal components below the waterline.

Anodes are cheap compared to the cost of replacing a damaged shaft, so it's good practice to just change them every time you get the opportunity.

Propeller and Shaft Maintenance

One of the places that you just can't avoid having a hole in your boat is where the shaft comes out. There are various schemes for sealing this hole against water intrusion. Some, like the dripless shaft seals, do not require maintenance (but do need to be regularly inspected—you can do so from inside the boat while it's in the water, however). Others, like traditional flax packing, wear thin and begin to leak and must be replaced.

Although it's possible to do this while the boat is in the water, it's much easier when it is out and you're not dealing with a constant stream of water while you're trying to repack it.

You'll need to consult the directions for your particular type of seal for details. Some rudder shafts use similar types of seals and should also be inspected and maintained at haulout.

You should also take the opportunity to inspect the exterior of the shaft and the cutless bearing where it exits the boat. You won't be able to see much of this, just the exterior face, but you may be able to spot signs of wear. You can also jiggle the shaft to judge the amount of play… tolerances are different on different vessels, but too much wiggle likely means the bearing is worn and needs to be replaced.

Propellers are pretty low-maintenance unless you are a sailor with a fancy folding prop, which may need to be lubricated. Again, this is an easy task that should be done every time the boat is out of the water.

Zinc-based spray paint is easy to apply to all types of propellers.

Since your shaft and propeller are probably metal and your hull probably isn't, you aren't likely to use the same type of paint on them, if you paint them at all. But in addition to shaft anodes, zinc spray paint is now available that can be used on most metal propellers to reduce the likelihood of galvanic corrosion. You do not want to apply *any* paint between a zinc and the shaft—metal to metal contact is vital for providing protection. Similarly, don't paint over the anodes.

Thru-hull Lubrication

Often overlooked is the necessity of lubricating thru-hull valves. Many of these are not exercised regularly and therefore are more prone to seizing up than other valves. And you do not want an underwater fitting that you cannot close on your boat!

Properly disassembling and lubricating the most common types of thru-hulls is a fairly laborious task. It should be done every few years, but there is a lazy lubber's method that can be performed quickly on any haulout and will help extend the life of the valve.

It's a two-person process. The person on the outside should get a glob of your preferred lubricant on a long brush that will fit up into the thru-hull from the exterior. The person on the interior will close the valve while the person outside shoves the lube up the hole. When it hits the closed valve, the inside person should work the valve handle a few times to spread the grease around.

The whole process should be repeated from the interior (only one person is necessary) with the hose removed to coat the other side of the valve.

This is not a replacement for full maintenance but, again, it's a quick and easy way to prolong the life of your equipment.

Living Aboard

Living aboard a boat is an acquired taste in the first place and not everyone takes to it like a duck to water. It's a rewarding, but hard, lifestyle.

One of the things that can make it hard is the necessity of hauling out every few years. Suddenly, your floating home is as landlocked as any lubber's nest. All the best parts of life on the water are left behind and you're stuck with only the bad parts, plus a few more:

- You're going have to climb a ladder anytime you need in or out.
- You're not going to be able to use your head or sinks.
- You may be stuck at a funny angle depending on how you are blocked up.

Crawling up and down a ladder to get to the head, brush your teeth, or take a shower several times a day gets old pretty fast. Faster, if you're of a certain age and have multiple head calls in the night.

Not a few boatyard liveaboards go the bucket route for such needs. Some even go so far as to bring a porta-potty on board.

Cooking is usually possible, but dishes are difficult without the ability to use the sink—dropping greywater out the bottom of the hull is frowned upon. Some intrepid liveaboards use disinfecting wipes on less messy dishes. Otherwise, you can invest in a tub and join the after-dinner procession to the yard restrooms to do the dishes there.

You're also living in a construction zone. In addition to the work you are doing on your own boat, which might create even more complications than just being on the hard, you are also going to be surrounded by dozens of other construction projects in progress. You will get full volume exposure to a wide variety of power tools during daylight hours and sometimes well into the night. Noxious fumes from epoxies and solvents will waft in through the ventilators. So will a lot of dirt, dust, and sand. If you're particularly unlucky, land-borne insects and rodents will also drop in for a visit.

Depending on the length and location of the haulout, you might be able to find some friends to crash with. If the yard is far from home or the work will take months not weeks, liveaboards have been known to spring for a hotel room rather than undergo the indignities of life on the hard.

CHAPTER NINE

Contingencies

No matter how complete your checklists, how copious your supplies, how thoughtful your planning, at some point you are going to run into something unexpected. Indeed, this is so likely that the entire art of the haulout might be considered as the practice of dealing with unexpected contingencies.

Although contingencies themselves, by their very nature, may not be a part of your plans, your plans can be vital in dealing with them. "Plans are worthless," Eisenhower is supposed to have said on the eve of D-day. "Planning is everything."

Like all military men, Ike knew that no plan ever survived contact with the enemy. But he also knew that, having gone through the planning process, his generals would have become familiar with conditions in the field and have thought about some alternatives if their original plans ended up in the shredder.

Likewise, the planning process is what will help you prepare for things going wrong, even if those things make your plans obsolete.

The Venerable Plan B

If Plan A is what you hope and have plotted to accomplish, Plan B is what you can actually get done in the time allotted after all the trials and vicissitudes of the boatyard harshly intrude. Both for practical and psychological purposes, it's a good idea to think through your Plan B in almost as much detail as Plan A. You won't be caught flat-footed when things go wrong.

Things you need to think about:
- Rain
- Broken tools or equipment
- Wrong parts or supplies ordered
- Contractor emergencies

You should also plan in the other direction: if great good fortune strikes and you get everything you wanted to do done ahead of schedule, is there anything else you can take on more easily while you're in the yard? If you put together the lists as suggested in Chapter 4 - Planning, you should have a few projects ready to go. Get your money's worth out of that yard time!

The easiest way to get a solid Plan B is to have a thorough Plan A (this was Eisenhower's point): by thinking through, step-by-step, what you intend to do, you will see more clearly both what can go wrong during those steps, and what your alternatives will be for handling those problems.

A simple example may be dealing with rain, the bane of the boat bottom-painter.

Say you have a three-day haulout scheduled. You have to prep the bottom (1 day), repair some dents you acquired in your keel by inadvertently using it as a depth sounder last season (1 day), and paint the entire bottom (1 day). The natural course of things might lead you to proceed in exactly that order. But what if Day 3 ends up turning into a monsoon?

You have a couple of options.

One is to alter your Plan A. Although bottom prep and keel repair both necessarily precede painting, it's not necessary to paint everything at once. Perhaps, to give yourself a buffer, you do your bottom prep on day 1, but then plan to do most of the painting—all but the keel—on day 2. Both repair and painting of the keel can happen on day 3 even if it rains since the keel is largely sheltered beneath the boat. If day 2 brings rain, your Plan B is to then go ahead with the keel work on that day and slip the painting to day 3.

Another option is to stick to the original prep/repair/paint schedule, but purchase material and hardware to put up a tent on day 3 if it looks like you are going to get washed out. In fact, since there's no guarantee that a storm on day 2 will abate by day 3, maybe that's your best Plan B, anyway.

The example is, of course, simplified and overly dramatic, but represents the sort of thinking you should do when you are putting your plans together.

Plan Z: Bail Out

Of course, you can't have a contingency plan for everything, and even plans B through Y can fall through. So at some point, you also have to think about Plan Z: put the sucker back in the water without everything done.

This is not only common but can also be desirable. Nothing balloons boatyard costs like unexpected projects. Having the discipline to avoid getting sucked into them, where possible, is a valuable quality.

You must, of course, adhere to rule one: don't go back in the water with unplugged holes in the bottom of the boat. But apart from that, nothing is going to be a complete disaster if you have to skip it and wait for the next opportunity.

Some things, usually safety related, may be worth a delay. Corroded keel bolts, for instance, might not immediately sink the boat when she is splashed, but it's only a matter of time.

Other items might simply be cheaper to do during this haulout rather than waiting for the next. Anything that required major disassembly to get at, for instance, might be easier to fix while you're already out and have things taken apart than waiting and going through the process of hauling and taking it all apart again. Even if it's more expensive than planned, it could be cheaper in the long run.

But don't dive into new projects without making those calculations. Think hard about making some notes and leaving the unexpected for the next round. You'll be out on the hard again soon enough.

PART FOUR

Splash

CHAPTER TEN

Splash, Don't Sink

It will either seem to come too soon or like it takes forever to arrive, but sooner or later the fateful day will arrive: your scheduled splash date!

"Splash," of course, is an overly dramatic description of what you hope will be a nice gentle landing back in the water. And it will probably be more of a relief than a cause for excitement.

To make sure that's the case, there are a few basic things you should do to prepare.

Clean Up

Both your yard space and the boat itself will probably be a little bit of a mess toward the end of your stay. Allot some time to get both of them cleaned up before you go back in the water.

If you were doing the work yourself, the yard will probably require that you dispose of any trash or junk left over from projects and return the space to the same basic state it was in when you arrived. Most yards have appropriate places to dispose of the various toxic and recyclable materials involved in boat projects. You should scout these out and make sure you understand the categories into which discards should be sorted so you can be bagging it appropriately before disposal.

Some yards also have places where you can donate unused materials to future haulees. Getting rid of some zincs that aren't in that bad shape? Have a gallon of leftover paint you didn't need? If you see any boats around that have rainbow striped bottoms, they probably got their paint out of the donations bin. Do your part and add any leftovers you may have to the bin.

There may be a limited amount of cleaning you can do on the boat itself. Many yards have prohibitions on using water for cleaning outside of the carefully managed wash-down pit—they need to manage potential pollutants in runoff (it's unclear why you should be allowed to spray this stuff off directly overboard when you get back in the water, but there you are).

Still, you can sweep, vacuum, and Windex to your heart's content. More importantly, you can put things away—get the deck and interior tidy again so you won't be tripping over stuff when you get back to the dock and so you can get at tools in a hurry if you have to.

Do not, however, secure any compartments that you will need to access to inspect the interior portion of any possible new leaks you may have created in the course of your projects. You will want to check them when the outside of the hull gets wet.

Diving In

The yard crew will take care of all the important steps for getting your baby back in the water safely. They will probably simply mirror the process used for pulling her out in the first place. As with your haulout, don't be late for your splash date— check in with the office early in the day to be sure they are ready and to let them know you are ready, and be near the boat itself ahead of the appointed hour.

Don't forget your usual seamanlike preparations for getting under way just because you're starting out from dry land rather than your slip—get your mooring lines rigged (both sides, to be safe) and fenders ready to deploy (ditto). Get out a boat hook and put it somewhere secure but handy… you can find yourself lurching around a little bit when they put you back in, and maneuvering room is usually tight.

After she is safely in the slings or forks, you may be given some time for last minute paint touch-ups or to perform other tasks you couldn't do while she was blocked—be ready to move quickly!

Make a last-minute survey of your thru-hulls and of any work you might have performed with the potential to compromise the watertight integrity of the hull. Double-check everything. Make sure your engine cooling thru-hull is open so you can start the boat safely when you are in the water, but close off the rest. If possible, leave open all your interior bilge access points! If water starts coming in, you want to know about it quickly.

Follow the instructions of the yard workers carefully, particularly with respect to the motor. Engaging your prop at the wrong instance can wreck it or the lift.

Once you are back in the water, most operators will leave you floating in the slings for a few moments. This is your opportunity to go below and make sure you aren't going to sink. Again, check thru-hulls that you may have worked on. Wooden boats, which may have dried out a bit and sprung their seams, will inevitably leak when they go back in no matter what, but you should be able to tell if anything unusual is going on. If there's a problem, don't hesitate to tell the yard workers! It's less embarrassing to get yanked back out than to sink as soon as you clear the lift.

Slipping The Date

Sometimes, despite all your efforts and best intentions, you just aren't quite ready to go back in when your scheduled date arrives. Slipping your splash date is liable to cost a little money, but it may be worth it to get your important projects finished.

In some yards, it's no big deal. They have the room or haulout capacity to keep you on the hard as long as you like and put you back in whenever is convenient (so long as you keep paying your bill!).

Other places, which may be booked more tightly, might levy an additional surcharge if you are taking up space that someone else had already scheduled. And if the lift schedule is busy, if you miss your appointment you could be waiting a long time for the next one. Even if you only need two more days to finish up, you might find that there is no slot for the lift available for another month! In those cases, you will have to choose between the additional lay-day costs you will incur and the benefit of getting all your projects finished up on this particular haulout.

In some cases, it's better to just go back in the water and plan to catch up on your projects on the next round. If you have planned appropriately and performed your projects in order of importance, then anything unfinished is likely to be a low priority anyway... it can likely wait a year or two for the next haulout.

Well-earned tranquility with a freshly waxed hull after a hard haulout..

Appendix: Common Yard Tasks

This list isn't intended to be an exhaustive list of every possible system to check on board when you are due for a haulout—that could easily be shortened to just "everything"—but more as a focused list of keywords that will hopefully prompt you to think about details of your own personal boat that could most easily be checked while it is out of the water. Read through it, see if it sparks any thoughts about things to check that you hadn't already thought about.

- Fuel tanks
    - Exterior (Corrosion, leaks)
    - Interior (Inspect for sludge)
- Holding tanks (inspect discharges and pumps)
- Hoses
- Hull
    - Blister repair
    - Bottom painting
    - Paying and caulking
    - Scraping/Cleaning
- Topsides cleaning, painting, waxing
- Keel
    - Check and tighten bolts
    - Hull/keel join sealing
- Propeller maintenance
    - Zincs/Paint/Lubrication
- Rudder maintenance
    - Seal
    - Bearings
- Shaft maintenance
    - Zincs

- Shaft seal
- Cutless bearing inspection
- Thru-hull maintenance
  - Lubrication
  - Check screens

Appendix: Pre-Haulout Checklist

Preparation is key to a smooth and happy haulout. You can prepare your boat for an easy round-trip through the yard by clearing the decks (literally and figuratively) to make her ready for work before you get up on the blocks.

- Clean and stow the interior
    - Remove as many items as possible
- If access will be necessary to parts of the hull interior (valves, hoses, etc) be especially sure to clear those areas.
- Check out the boatyard
    - If possible, check the location they will put you
- Consider emptying fuel and water tanks to reduce weight
- Remove food
- Remove any vulnerable transducers
- Remove sails
- Secure deck for sea
- Ensure tools you may need are easy to access
- Keep bottom photos or diagram handy for reference
- Lock rudder and propeller
- Close and secure bilge/blackwater discharges
- Close all portholes and hatches

Appendix: Pre-Splash Checklist

Hopefully you won't be completely frazzled and out of sorts by the time you get to the end of your haulout, but just in case you're not thinking straight after a week of inhaling bottom paint fumes, this is a basic list of all-important items to check before they drop your boat back in the drink.

- Check your yard space
    - Clean-up
    - Collect tools and gear
- Check all thru-hulls
    - Hoses on and secure
    - Valves to correct position (engine cooling intake, for example, should be open)
- Check them again!
- Clean up
- Secure deck and interior for sailing
    - …except leave clear any spaces necessary to quickly check if yard projects are leaking!
- Check all tape or temporary gear below waterline removed
- Attach docklines—both sides, fore and aft
- Rig fenders to be deployed quickly
- Get a boathook ready

Glossary

Amidships - The middle of the boat, conventionally as judged between bow and stern; however, may also mean the centerline between both beams.

Aft - At or toward the stern of the boat.

Ballast - Weight carried on a boat for purposes of increasing stability in the water.

Beam - The measure of the boat's width at the widest portion or the direction relative to that portion.

Berth - (see also Sea Berth, Pilot Berth, V-berth, Quarterberth) An accommodation in which to sleep on board the boat. Some berths may be fixed in place, as with v-berths or bunks, while others may be converted from other components, such as settees or tables which convert into sleeping locations.

Blackwater - Sewage or other waste water from toilets (see also Head).

Bow - The front, or foremost part of the boat.

Bulkhead - A dividing wall between compartments in the boat.

Bung - A stopper, such as a cork or wood plug, used to plug up a hole.

Bridge - The elevated deck on a boat from which it may be steered or commanded. Common to powerboats but unusual on modern sailing vessels.

Cabin - A room inside a boat partitioned off by bulkheads from other interior spaces.

Cockpit - The well on a boat where the helm station is located. On sailboats, this space is commonly where access to the interior is gained, and is usually furnished with benches and designed for outside entertainment. (see also Bridge).

Displacement - The weight of the amount of water pushed away when a boat is floating in it. This is also the weight of the boat itself, but displacement is often used as a theoretical measurement discounting current lading.

Draft - The depth of water to which the bottommost portion of the boat extends.

Fiddle - A vertical lip or fixture attached to the edge of a table or counter and designed to prevent items from falling off when the boat is in motion.

Forward - At or toward the bow of the boat.

Galley - The kitchen or cooking space aboard the boat.

Graywater - Non-sewage waste water, typically from sinks or showers.

Halyard - A line to the top of the mast, used to hoist sails or other flags or equipment.

Head - A marine toilet, or the compartment on board which contains the toilet.

Helm - The steering station on the boat.

Holding Tank - A container on board designed to hold waste water until it can be safely and legally disposed of. Commonly for blackwater but increasingly used for graywater holding in some areas.

Lazarette - A small compartment at or near the stern of the vessel, commonly housing the steering gear but frequently used for the storage of equipment or mechanical gear.

Length - The longitudinal measurement from bow to stern at the longest point of the boat.

   On Deck - Length on Deck (LOD) refers to the length of the vessel on the main deck from bow to stern. Does not include overhangs such as rails, anchors, or sprits.

   Overall - Theoretically, Length Overall (LOA) measures the length of the vessel including fixtures fore and aft of the deck, such as bowsprits, davits, and so forth. Sometimes this measurement is made discounting anchors or other equipment overhanging permanent fixtures. In such cases, the total, complete length of the vessel including both temporary and permanent extensions may be referred to as the Extreme Length of Vessel (ELOV) when that figure is required.

Waterline - The Waterline Length (LWL) measures the length of the vessel at the point where it sits in the water at the designed displacement.

Locker - A compartment accessible from inside or outside the boat in which equipment may be stowed.

'Midships - See "Amidships"

Macerator - A mechanical device which may be used in marine heads to chop up waste before transferring it to a holding tank or disposing of it overboard; helps prevent clogs in the sewage system.

Mast - A vertical spar, usually used to carry sails on sailboats, but often also present on powerboats and used as a platform for antennas, lights, and tackle for hoisting gear or tenders on board.

Mooring - 1. A fixed anchoring point in a harbor where a vessel can be secured without deploying her own anchors. Usually marked by a buoy. 2. Commonly used to describe the act of securing a vessel in any location, whether at a mooring or at a dock or pier.

Navigation Desk - Or "Nav Desk," a flat or inclined table on the boat designed to provide a position at which charts may be spread out and calculations made for navigating the vessel. Frequently also the location where electronics and the main electrical panel for the boat are located.

Overhead - The ceiling of a cabin, or the top surface in any enclosed compartment on the boat.

Pilot Berth - A bunk typically set into the sides of the main cabin on sailboats. Frequently used as shelf or storage space.

Port - 1. The left-hand side of the boat when viewed aft to fore. Also "Larboard" in older use. 2. A harbor in which ships may be moored or serviced.

Quarter - 1. The two after parts of the ship to either side of the centerline; hence "port quarter" and "starboard quarter." 2. The direction given on the approximate bearing away from the boat along the same lines.

Quarterberth - A berth usually oriented fore and aft and located in either quarter. Typically smaller than a v-berth but often a better sea-berth. Due to the location below and beside the cockpit in many designs, the overhead is usually low and access is restricted, leaving many liveaboards to relegate quarterberths to a storage, rather than sleeping, role.

Salon - Or "Saloon." The main cabin in the boat, used for eating or entertaining. In many small boats, the only cabin apart from the head.

Sea Berth - A berth specially designed to secure the occupant while the boat is in motion. Typically equipped with lee cloths, rectangular panels of fabric which are secured at the corners to provide a soft surface for the sleeper to roll against when the vessel rolls or lurches.

Settee - A long, upholstered or cushioned seat accommodating multiple people. In many small boats, settees represent the main seating in the salon as well as convertible berths.

Spar - A stout pole of some sort; generically describes masts, yards, gaffs, booms and other various appendages of the boat.

Starboard - The right-hand side of the boat when viewed aft to fore.

Stem - The foremost structural member at the bow of the vessel.

Stern - The back-most part of the vessel.

Stow - The act of stowing, or putting away, items or equipment.

Stowage - The space or manner of stowing something.

Thru-hull - A hole penetrating through the hull of the boat; thru-hulls below the waterline are often controlled with valves (called seacocks) to allow them to be closed

V-berth - A roughly triangular shaped berth, typically in the bows, which often represents the largest and "master" accommodations on board small boats. The unusual shape can make the accommodation difficult to make up.

Well-found - Properly equipped and maintained for the purpose at hand.

More Books For Lubbers

For more information about haulouts, including personal stories, updates, and regional resources, see our website at http://haulingout.forlubbers.com!

Need a little more nautical knowledge? Check out…
Lubber's Guides

Because everybody is a lubber sometimes…

So our nautical guidebooks cover the topics that others just assume you already understand. We use fun, plain language to explain the basics of elementary boat-buying, boat-handling, and boat-keeping skills that every mariner and boat owner needs to know.

If you're interested in other fun, easy-to-understand explanations on a variety of nautical subjects, check out http://www.forlubbers.com to check out our other books!

Living Aboard: The Ultimate Guide to Life on a Boat
Everybody wants to live the dream! Learn about life on board, from selecting the right boat to downsizing to finding the right place to stay.

Buying A Boat… Everything You Need To Know To Go Shopping For The Boat Of Your Dreams

Before you can haul it out, you have to buy it, right? Don't get stuck with a lemon that will leave you in the lurch in the yard... read this quick and easy-to-understand guide to boat shopping and purchase!

Lazarette - Boomkin - Chine

What are these three words? Well, don't worry about them right now, all right? We'll let you know what to do with them later... keep an eye on our website or follow us on Twitter.

www.ingramcontent.com/pod-product-compliance
Lightning Source LLC
Chambersburg PA
CBHW071849020426
42331CB00007B/1931